VOLUME 100 OF THE YALE SERIES OF YOUNGER POETS

GREEN SQUALL

JAY HOPLER

FOREWORD BY LOUISE GLÜCK

YALE UNIVERSITY PRESS

NEW HAVEN AND LONDON

Designed by Nancy Ovedovitz and set in Electra type
by Integrated Publishing Solutions. Printed in the
United States of America.

Library of Congress Cataloging-in-Publication Data
Hopler, Jay, 1970–
Green squall / Jay Hopler ; foreword by Louise Glück.
     p.   cm. — (Yale series of younger poets ; v. 100)
Includes bibliographical references.
ISBN-13: 978-0-300-11453-9 (cloth : alk. paper)
ISBN-13: 978-0-300-11454-6 (pbk. : alk. paper)
ISBN-10: 0-300-11453-2 (cloth : alk. paper)
ISBN-10: 0-300-11454-0 (pbk. : alk. paper)
I. Title.   II. Series.
PS3608.O658G74   2006
811'.6—dc22
2005024636

A catalogue record for this book is available from the
British Library.

The paper in this book meets the guidelines for
permanence and durability of the Committee on
Production Guidelines for Book Longevity of the
Council on Library Resources.

10   9   8   7   6   5   4   3   2   1

for my father and mother, with love and gratitude

Gardens of strange adventure;
Distortion; gruesome flower-masks, laughter,
monsters,
And rolling constellations in the dark briars.

— Georg Trakl

CONTENTS

Before poetry began pitching its tents in the library and
museum, before, that is, mediated experience supplanted
what came to seem the naive fantasy of more direct encounter,
a great many poems began in the garden.

In the tense final decades of the twentieth century, poets have
tended to treat the natural world as a depleted or exhausted
metaphor: the old associations, continuity and renewal, like
other emblems of hope, seem poignantly remote. Nor do artists
seem tempted to resurrect them—they hardly lend themselves
to the prevailing tone, to the particular set of tools a generation
has systematically developed and enshrined, tools developed to
address other kinds of experiences than those nature is presumed
to afford. If, recently, disinterest has given way to fierce steward-
ship as the environment grows more and more imperiled, if
nature threatened and uncertain has been restored to a certain
dignity as the mirror of our own precariousness, if the throwback
has become the harbinger, the problem of tone still remains.
The vanishing garden currently revived by poets suits a period
in which experience is filtered, prismatically, by art and history:
it is not so much a real garden as a garden previously real. The

inauthentic present suggesting the charged and important past insofar as irony permits.

Irony has become less part of a whole tonal range than a scrupulous inhibiting armor, the disguise by which one modern soul recognizes another. In contemporary practice, it is characterized by acute self-consciousness without analytic detachment, a frozen position as opposed to a means of inquiry. Essential, at every moment, to signal that one knows one is not the first to think or feel what one thinks or feels. This stance is absolutely at odds with the actual sensations of feeling, certainly, as well with the sensations of making—the sense, immediate and absolute, of unprecedented being, the exalted intensification of that fundamental isolation which marks all things mortal.

Green Squall begins and ends in a garden. But no one would mistake Jay Hopler for a poet of another century: he is more mad scientist than naturalist, his exploding Florida garden a formidable outpost of the seasonal garden of English lyric. If the seasonal garden represents cyclical time (the old ideas of renewal and so on), Hopler's obsession is with entropy, its symbol, often, unremitting fertility:

> And the sky!
> Nooned with the steadfast blue enthusiasm
> Of an empty nursery.
>
> Crooked lizards grassed in yellow shade.
>
> The grass was lizarding,
> Green and on a rampage. . . .

So the book starts. But "begins and ends" seem the wrong terms—
Green Squall hardly ever leaves its fertile premises. Hard, though,
to equal all that flourishing:

1

There is a hole in the garden. It is empty. I envy it.

Emptiness: the only freedom there is
In a fallen world.

2

Father Sunflower, forgive me—. I have been so preoccupied
       with my backaches and my headaches,
With my sore back and my headaches and my beat-skipping
       heart,

I have ignored the subtle huzzah of the date palms and
       daisies, of the blue daze and the date palms—

3

                         Or don't forgive me, what do I
                             care?
I am tired of asking for forgiveness; I am tired of being
       frightened all the time.
I want to run down the street with a vicious erection,
Impaling everything, screaming obscenities
And flapping my arms; *fuck the date palms,*
Fuck the daisies—

4

As a man, I am a disappointment, I know that.
Is it my fault I was born in shadow? Through the banyan
       trees,

An entourage of slovenly blondes
Comes naked and begging—

5

My days fly from me as though from a murderer.
Can you blame them?

Behind us, the house is empty and quiet as light.

What have I done, Mother,
That I should spend my life
Alone?

Insouciance and bravura notwithstanding, there is a solitude in this art as deep as any in American poetry since Stevens. For all the explosive vitality and wild fantasy, there are almost no people here. The mother who periodically figures is like Ramon Fernandez in Stevens's "The Idea of Order at Key West": from neither is response expected. Ghostly, remote, part imagination, part memory: behind the appeals and questions to such figures, another larger question lurks. Beneath "tell me if you know," the echoing "tell me that you *are*, that you exist."

Stevens, the great master of tropical extrapolation, is the presiding influence. Like Stevens, Hopler combines verbal extravagance and formal invention with the philosopher's profound inwardness. In *Green Squall*, inwardness is manifest: even the garden is a courtyard. Impossible, here, not to think of the place where prisoners take their exercise. Despite violent flourishing, Hopler's courtyard is a kind of prison, a place of voluntary entrapment or exile; its occupants aspire to invisibility. As a place, as an idea, utterly distinct from the hospitable earth of sentimental practice.

Hopler's real companions are other forms of life: flowers, dogs, birds. His flowers have an energy the speaker envies, as he envies their resilient obliviousness. Hopler is as far from unconsciousness as any poet I can name, despite his relentless efforts to intensify sensory deprivation. But at least once, the courtyard affords the serenity that is the aim of self deprivation, justifying the speaker's obstinate retreat:

> This morning, still
> And warm, heavy with the smells
>
> Of gardenia and Chinese wisteria,
> The first few beams of spring sun-
>
> Light filtering through the flower-
> Crowded boughs of the magnolia,
>
> I cannot conceive a more genuine,
> More merciful, form of happiness
>
> Than solitude.

More commonly, the view is less sanguine as in these two sections from the long poem at the center of the book:

6

We Cannot Love the World as It Is

> We cannot love the world as it is,
> Because the world, as it is, is impossible to love.
>
> We have only to lust for it—
> To lust for each other in it—
>
> And, somehow, to make that suffice.

7

Revisited

> No, somehow to make *that sacrifice.*

Repeatedly one sees in the stanzas—sometimes even in the phrases—a characteristic psychological progression, most marked in poems of real gusto and high spirits: the initial spurt of energy and animal vigor yields almost immediately to morose woe. Euphoria seems less a precursor of depression than a component of being depressed. Anxiety either aborts or trumps it, the danger of euphoria being how much noise it makes: it threatens to reveal the soul's hiding place. Hopler's stanzas are like runners who charge the starting gate and then, two feet later, sit down in the dust. But the variations within this structure, in poem after poem, are extraordinary. What is more extraordinary, however, is that irony and self-consciousness, both taken to extremes, have not suppressed intensity. Nor has Hopler's devastating bitter wit, his Larkinesque crankiness, suppressed amazing verbal beauty.

His tonal range, like his range of formal strategies, is immense. How exhilarating to discover, in a long-winded period, a poet with this genius for epigram. A number of poems in *Green Squall* do not exceed six lines; others are made up of linked epigrams, bleak pensées connected together in one varied glittering comic gesture. "The Frustrated Angel," for example, with its sly self-contained jibes and deadpan remarks:

> The Angel says I have the quiet confidence and smoldering
> Good looks one usually associates with more confident and
>   attractive people.
>
> A coward's confession—, that's what he thinks my ulcer is. . . .

And, later,

*That's mighty big talk, isn't it, Hopler—coming from a man
who lives with his mother?*

Reprimand and regret weave through these poems like dark
thread. Fantasies of erasure alternate with visions of stasis: Hopler
broods over the present as one broods over a diagnosis—it con-
firms the past as it predicts the future's cold encroaching certain-
ties. But the major mistakes have all been made, the first having
been the most dire:

1

Being born is a shame—

But it's not so bad, as journeys go. It's not the worst one
We will ever have to make. It's almost noon

And the light now clouded in the courtyard is
Like that light one finds in baby pictures: old

And pale and hurt—

and, later,

3

The clouded light has changed to rain.
The picture—. No, *the baby's* blurry.

Green Squall is a book filled with tardy recognitions and in-
sights. Always we sense, beneath the surface of even the most
raucous poems, impending crisis: the terrifying onset of that life
long held at a distance. Always bravura is connected to melan-
choly, fastidious distinctions to wild exuberance, largesse to
connoisseurship, self-contempt to uncontrollably erupting

hopefulness. Hopler's dreamy obscurities and rapturous effusions share with his more direct speech a refusal to be groomed into uncommunicative cool: they are encoded, not unintelligible. He writes like someone haunted or stalked; he wants, simultaneously, to hide and to end the anxiety of hiding, to reveal himself (in every sense of the word), to give himself away.

Like all art that has a chance to be remembered, *Green Squall* is an account of being. Such helpless authenticity seems rare now. But perhaps it has always been rare. Perhaps it is more accurate to say that the ratio of competent verse to art has, in our time, shifted. Jay Hopler sounds like no one else: there is a kind of dazed surprise in the lines, as though the poet himself didn't know where these riches came from. And excitement of the highest order: you could no more sleep through Hopler than you could sleep through an alarm clock—the pleasure, of course, is hardly comparable. Like all artists, Jay Hopler writes not to report or re-create experience but to create forms that both enact and define it:

1
Not enough effort in the sky for morning.
The only relics left are those long,

Blunt fingers among the multitudinous buds.
How hard it is, we say—

The will to work is laid aside.

2
I have reached no conclusions, have erected no boundaries.
I have rested, drooling at the mouth-hole.

I have imagined bees coming and going.
I have said that the soul is not more than the body.

I've melted my silver for you.
I have strewn the leaf upon the sod.

I have just come down from my father.
I have suffered, in a dream, because of him.

3
Suddenly from all the green in the park,
A small white envelope appears.

As limpid, dense twilight comes,
The center of its patch of darkness, sparkling,

Rises like a moon made of black glass.
Beneath the clouds the low sky glows—

The garden that was never here,
Reveal it to me. . . .

Louise Glück

ACKNOWLEDGMENTS

Grateful acknowledgment is made to the editors of the periodicals in which some of these poems, sometimes in different forms, first appeared:

> *Boulevard:* "Meditation on a Blue Vase"; *Colorado Review:* "Approaching the Tower," "Of Paradise," "With Both Eyes Closing"; *Eclipse:* "In the Time of Dreary Miracles"; *Gulf Coast:* "Of Passion and Seductive Trees"; *The Iowa Review:* "Green Squall," "The Howling of the Gods"; *The Journal:* "Like the Stare of Some Glass-Eyed God"; *Mid-American Review:* "And the Sunflower Weeps for the Sun, Its Flower"; *The New Yorker:* "That Light One Finds in Baby Pictures"; *Pleiades:* "The Frustrated Angel," "Nothing to Do Now but Sit and Wait," "Of the Dead So Much Less Is Expected," "Out of These Wounds, the Moon Will Rise"; *Ploughshares:* "In the Garden," "Meditation on Beethoven: Symphony 9"; *POOL:* "The Boxcars of Consolidated Rail Freight"; *Puerto del Sol:* "Meditation on Ruin"; *Sonora Review:* "Joy on the Edge of Vertigo"; *Xantippe:* "The Wildflower Field"

I wish to thank Louise Glück, Kimberly Johnson, Dana Levin, John Kulka, and the teachers with whom it was my privilege to study at both the Johns Hopkins University Writing Seminars and the Iowa Writers' Workshop.

PART 1

IN THE GARDEN

And the sky!
Nooned with the steadfast blue enthusiasm
Of an empty nursery.

Crooked lizards grassed in yellow shade.

The grass was lizarding,
Green and on a rampage.

Shade tenacious in the crook of a bent stem.

Noon. This noon —
Skyed, blue and full of hum, full of bloom.
The grass was lizarding.

OF PARADISE

There is a black fly drowning in that glass of beer.
There is a black fly drowning in that glass of beer.

How can no one notice it,
That black fly?

Black as a zero is useless.
Black as grammar school.

The man with the beer is a fisherman,
Small and gigantic

In his white rubber boots.
How sick we are, the three of us,

Of Paradise.

THAT LIGHT ONE FINDS IN BABY PICTURES

1

Being born is a shame —

But it's not so bad, as journeys go. It's not the worst one
We will ever have to make. It's almost noon

And the light now clouded in the courtyard is
Like that light one finds in baby pictures: old

And pale and hurt —

2

When all roads are low and lead to the same
Place, we call it *Fate* and tell ourselves how

We were born to make the journey. Who's
To say we weren't?

3

The clouded light has changed to rain.
The picture — . No, *the baby's* blurry.

4

That's me —, the child playing in the sand with a pail
And shovel; in the background, my mother's shadow

Is crawling across a soot-blackened collapse of brick
And timber, what might have been a bathhouse once.

The tide is coming in —. Someone has written HELL
On its last standing wall.

WITH BOTH EYES CLOSING

1

How high and white the moon!
And vampired — .

    Like the light a child
Sinking sees.

A child pushed by its mother
Through the hole in the ice.

2

Are there daffodils
In that vase . . .

    Yellow daffodils
In that blue

Vase? Are there spiders
In the corners,

    In the corn-
Ices,

    The eaves?

3

If I am sinking, how comes it I can breathe?

4

If I put a daffodil
In that vase,

    A single yellow daffodil
In that blue

Vase —. No,
That moon

    Would still be useless.
Still useless.

    Like the human race.

5

What use is such a flimsy soul —

Let spiders suck the light of me
And silk it into corners!

    Tell me, Mother, truly —
What use is such a flimsy soul?

THE BOXCARS OF CONSOLIDATED RAIL FREIGHT

Those angels of history are whispering, again,
That I'm the product of two people who should have known
Better.

Now one of them is dying. The other is going
Crazy over it. I know — . To this day, there's a space behind

My eyes that stays lit like some small-town museum's North
Atlantic collection.

My thoughts: bird bones. In the mud.

If she's lucky, she'll come back whimpering,
With nothing but a limp: a yard hound with its muzzle split,

Roughly. By a board. But who among the living's counted
Lucky, anymore? Not my poor, grief-crazèd mother, that's
For sure.

I fear that, like Proserpine — whose husband,
Too, was underground — my mother will divided be 'tween
A world

Of the living and a world of the dead.

And — though her stays in each will be temporary — her loss
Will be perpetual. And profound.

THE HOWLING OF THE GODS

It was so loud it was so quiet we didn't sleep we slept.

We didn't dream. We dreamt of panthers and hatpins, orchids
    and ashbins.

There was no moon; no moon was there

Ever so magnificent. Even the dogs were mesmerized.

Make that: *the gods* — even *the gods* were mesmerized.

There were no dogs; no dogs were there.

Even so, sleep was impossible —

All that howling! We dreamt of panthers and hatpins, orchids
    and ashbins.

Didn't we? No; and if we did,

We weren't dreaming.

OF THE DEAD SO MUCH LESS IS EXPECTED

How delightful it would be to lie in bed and think of nothing
But how cool the sheets are and how hot it must be outdoors

This morning, the sky, loud-blue and cloudless, the sun now
Fully up. I only wish I could stop feeling sorry for the birds.

Not one decent splay of shade is there beneath these August-
Walloped trees — the birdbath: choked-out, cracked, a-wreck

With weeds —

                    I think I read somewhere that certain
Birds prefer a dust bath, but that seems a wretched comfort

On a day like this is shaping up to be; listen: the wind's not
Even moving the leaves around; the grass is growing brittle,

Giving up its green. Birds bursting into flame in mid-flight,
That's what I half-expect to see when I cross to the window —

The day cracking down the middle — falling into the weeds.

ACADEMIC DISCOURSE AT MIAMI: WALLACE STEVENS AND THE DOMESTICATION OF LIGHT

I have no beef with Wallace Stevens
Even if some of his poems do feel like so much tropical slumming.

I only wish he could have lived here, in Florida, instead of simply
Visiting once in a while — ; how much more essential his summer-

Minded poems would have been! Not that a poem like "Farewell
To Florida" is solely summer-minded or is, somehow, inessential —

Only, that there exists a difference between the tropical light one
Finds beaming in a Stevens poem and the tropical light one finds

Burning in the tropics. Florida's light is far more aggressive, far
More violent, than Stevens knew —

It gets inside your head and shreds
Things, dismantles memory, shorts out the will; even now, at six

O'clock of a Friday evening, the light here in Florida is clanging,
Banging, rattling buildings, burning through the park's green pelt.

This never happens in a Stevens poem.

MEDITATION ON RUIN

It's not the lost lover that brings us to ruin, or the barroom brawl,
     or the con game gone bad, or the beating
Taken in the alleyway. But the lost car keys,
The broken shoelace,
The overcharge at the gas pump
Which we broach without comment — these are the things that
     eat away at life, these constant vibrations
In the web of the unremarkable.

The death of a father — the death of the mother —
The sudden loss shocks the living flesh alive! But the broken
     pair of glasses,
The tear in the trousers,
These begin an ache behind the eyes.
And it's this ache to which we will ourselves
Oblivious. We are oblivious. Then, one morning — *there's a*
     crack in the water glass — we wake to find ourselves undone.

OUT OF THESE WOUNDS, THE MOON WILL RISE

Now that the sun has set and the rain has abated,
And every porch light

                       in the neighborhood is lit,
Maybe we can invent something; I'd like a new

Way of experiencing the world, a way of taking
Into myself the single light shining at the center

Of all things without losing the dense, eccentric
Planets orbiting around it.

                      What you'd like is a more
Attentive lover, I suppose — . Too bad that slow,

Wet scorch of orange blossoms floating towards
The storm drain is not a vein of stars . . . we could

Make a wish on one of them; not that we would
Wish for anything but the impossible.

IN THE TIME OF DREARY MIRACLES

1

in the time of dreary miracles — before the coming of moonlit
    humidors and prehistoric orchards
in the time of dreary miracles — before the coming of piebald
    lizards and succulent lumberyards
in the time of dreary miracles — before the coming of seismic
    pineapples and republican guitars
in the time of dreary miracles — before the coming of lissome
    picnics and translucent pubic hair

alcoholic trolley cars made love in glacial lakes

2

alcoholic trolley cars made love in glacial lakes — beware the
    sunburned humming birds!
glacial lakes made love in alcoholic trolley cars — beware the
    funereal ice cream parlors!

alcoholic trolley cars made love to glacial lakes — beware the
    ravenous avenues of glass!

glacial lakes made love to alcoholic trolley cars — beware the
   clairvoyant mooring buoy!

3

in the time of dreary miracles — before the coming of Gnostic
   frogmen and pornographic asphalt
in the time of dreary miracles — before the coming of contrite
   juggernauts and vestigial kimonos
in the time of dreary miracles — before the coming of strident
   vitamins and cloistered bartenders
in the time of dreary miracles — before the coming of languid
   hangmen and gratuitous rutabagas

mosquitoes were worshipped by biopsy needles

4

mosquitoes were worshipped by biopsy needles — beware the
   convoluted history of pins!
mosquitoes were worshipped by biopsy needles — beware the
   parenthetical glockenspiel!

mosquitoes were worshipped by biopsy needles — beware the
   obligatory kiss on the arm!
mosquitoes were worshipped by biopsy needles — beware the
   monochromatic jet stream!

APPROACHING THE TOWER

Light! Light! Light!

The stars tonight are like tinfoil fleas
On a black rat.

I'm here.
Not far from the train yards.
Not far from the river.

My eyes no less blue than they ever were.

Look in my mirror, Mother.
Tell me if my good
        Heart isn't bad luck.

Tonight, I'm no more resigned to light
Than some canary,
Its eyes pried open with pins.

How come more children
Don't mistake the river for a schoolyard,
        Dark as it is?

Nothing moving but the trains.

And the trees, so quiet.

Like towers.

Waiting for their snipers to arrive.

THE FRUSTRATED ANGEL

The Angel says if I want to be a sucker, that's my business,
But it's all about service, not servitude — in this world, you
Either become a monster or you wait on one.

O, Hopler! If only sitting on your hands was heroic! If only
boredom was a form of prayer!

The Angel says I have the quiet confidence and smoldering
Good looks one usually associates with more confident and
attractive people.

A coward's confession —, that's what he thinks my ulcer is.
He thinks I should knock some heads together if I'm really
So convinced everyone is such a mother-
Fucker.

I see what they mean, Hopler —

one really does get tired of you.

He wants to know how often I've been mistaken for a shrub.

The Angel says if you beat someone long enough and hard enough,
They will learn to love you for it.

That's mighty big talk, isn't it, Hopler — coming from a man who lives with his mother?

Hopler, I've had it with all your crying and complaining. If I wanted to hear whining, I'd kick a dog.

NOTHING TO DO NOW BUT SIT AND WAIT

1

A pair of African parakeets lands in the backyard
And vanishes, or seems to, because their feathers

Are a green that matches the grass almost exactly
And because the light by which the lawn is being

Lit is weaker than it used to be —

2

                             Last-legged,

A little closer to ghostly; a little closer to October
Than to April, actually —, though it's not quite as

Visibly bristled or as sharply defined. April's got
A way of doing that, slumming about in autumn's

Ragged clothes, throwing long, funereal shadows,
Taking shallow breaths —

3

       The parakeets are preening,
Plucking feathers from their breasts. The wind is

Bearing them away so quickly —, so quietly. It's
Like they were never here.

LITTLE MIRRORS OF DESPAIR

It is the end of a beautiful summer —.
It is going to rain and my mother is humming.

The closely cropped leaves of the boxwood reflect an oncoming
     moonlight; the breeze carries it across
The koi pond.

Is it really so bad, this garden with its koi fish ponded . . . its birds
     seed-fed . . . my mother humming —

Her voice so soft . . . , so far-off-hearted,
Like the sound of the grass lying down.

Couldn't we be happy
Here?

The rain is just beginning to fall.
The sky gives up its water like an old woman wringing
The life out of her son.

The drops hit the still surface of the koi pond
And shatter it, the ripples and rings sparkling

Like little moonlit
Mirrors of despair.

MEDITATION ON A BLUE VASE

I have a blue vase but no flowers.

I never have any flowers, not one of my neighbors has ever given
me flowers.

I keep an empty blue vase empty.

I should fill it. With what, white mice and charcoal?

I should fill it. With what, Chinese bees?

If I fill it, my estranged neighbor will give me flowers and I will
have no place to put them.

Should I fill it with red prawns and tobacco?

Should I fill it with my own gold teeth?

I have a blue vase but no flowers.

I have no flowers. My neighbor has them all.

LIKE THE STARE OF SOME GLASS-EYED GOD

If we are not busy fixing what we have broken, we are busy breaking
What, someday, we will need to fix.

As for that which cannot be broken —
As for that for which there is no fix —

                        I wish we were patches
Of that miraculous afternoon light:

Bright. Unbroken. Fixed
On the grass —

Imagine! Being fixed on the grass.
How sad . . . , what has come to pass

For the miraculous.

MEMOIR

Of the two undiscovered countries, Life and Death,
Which one lies the closer to God?

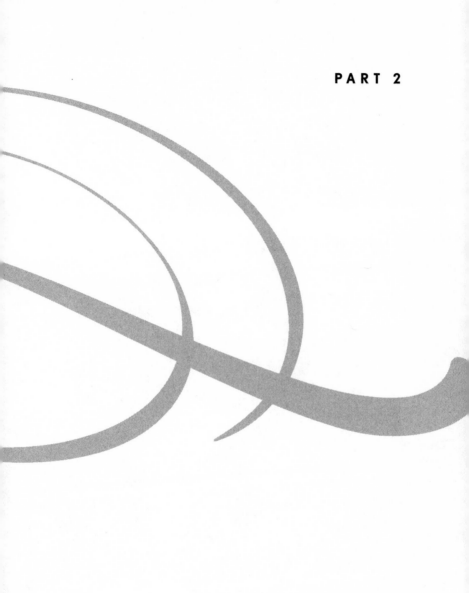

PART 2

OF HUNGER AND HUMAN FREEDOM

1

The Bird in the Courtyard

       Those whirls she trailed of red, flocked,
Cloth across the black macadam of the parking lot

Looked nothing like some trapped bird's fear-dropped feathers.
And yet, that's what I thought of when I saw her: that red bird in
    the courtyard,

Trapped — its feathers like scraps of red cloth
Dropping against the black mesh

Of the screen door. A cardinal, I think it was —
Lean and summer-hungry.

Revisited

Summer-hungry, can that be right?
I didn't think things went hungry in the summer.

3

The Woman in Red

She trailed across that parking lot
Such worlds of red — , it was as if the sky had taken off its hinges
    the last black door of winter and let go

A sigh, the first, long satisfied sigh of summer.
Satisfied — that can't be right; summer's never

Satisfied, never quite. It's never quiet, either; it doesn't sigh,
It cries. It howls. It bleats and groans. Its stomach growls —

The rookery islands and the mangrove strands,
The mossy hummocks and the season beaches,

Echo at all hours with the roiling,
Mad cacophonies of that longing.

4

The Courtyard

                Sitting in this courtyard, thinking of the bird
That was trapped here and the woman in red,

Listening to the tree frogs wring their rubber tongues in the
        moist air, breathing deep the heaving-green
Smell of the peat moss and the palm trees, watching the leaves
        of the mangos and the limes, the guavas,

Tremble, grow still — tremble and grow still —
You know what I long for?

An end to summer.

5

The Courtyard

Just imagine the peace in that quiet.

        And the clouds this morning!
Moving like a herd of curtains across a pasture of blue glass —

It would be a relief; no, it would be
A *release* —

      Not just *from* something, but *into* something,
Into the midst of something: a day endowed with summer's
Jungled lushness but lacking its lust —

Yes —, a lack of lust! That's what I
Long for. To live in the midst of the physical, the visceral,
Untroubled by the crush
Of want —

6

We Cannot Love the World as It Is

             We cannot love the world as it is,
Because the world, as it is, is impossible to love.

We have only to lust for it —
To lust for each other in it —

And, somehow, to make that suffice.

7

Revisited

No, somehow to make *that sacrifice.*

8

The Goddess of the Parking Lot

Maybe it was Ceres I saw that day,
Moving across that parking lot in breeze-blown blooms of red,
　　flocked, cloth and not just some woman who was
A credit to her dress. Unlikely, I admit — but wouldn't it
Make sense? In a world overrun with hunger engines whose
　　need to consume everything is bringing them, once again,
　　to the brink of their own extinction,
Where else but a parking lot — a used-up, paved-over field —
Would one expect to find a goddess
Of agriculture?

And one bedecked in red, no less!
Red — the color of passion, lust and blood — the color of war, not
　　wheat — the color of Mars with its two moons,
Deimos and Phobos, Panic and Fear, fixed in their morbid orbits.
Mars was the god of grain for a time, but he gave it up for war, a
　　growth industry —
He didn't see much future in fertility.
Poor Ceres — . Gone the blood route,
Too, I see.

Still — , she looked so beautiful
In that red dress. Even if it wasn't the one she was born to wear,
She made of it a fit, magnificent — an exquisiteness the fire-wild
　　billowings of which lit a day

Not otherwise enlightened and lifted from that place the gray
    weight of late-winter cloud cover, raising it above the
    streetlamps for the first time
In months. And whether she had come as feast or as famine —
In the name of war or wheat, I did not care — for the miracle
Of that dress alone would I have loved her.

Meditation on the Nature of Human Freedom

                          Our bonds are inescapable. Freedom's not
Our natural state, nor does it follow, naturally, the mere
      cessation of restraint. Even in the absence of our masters,
Are we mastered; even in the absence of the father, we wait
      upon the father upon whom have we waited our lives
Long. That wasn't Ceres I saw that day, gliding across
The parking lot in breeze-blown blooms of red-flocked
Cloth, but the daughter of Erysichthon,
Turning herself into a bird — a cardinal —
Her feathers billowing up in great red clouds around her as she
      moved across that parking lot.
She had no earthly reason to reenact those wrongs to which her
Father and her masters had subjected her; yet, she did just that.
      And when her transformation was complete,
She flew off not to seek her father's house — for she knew it to
      be ruined —
But to seek a place that would in ways
Approximate that prison. What brought her to *my* father's house,
I do not know. No place is there less prison-like
Than this; the rooms are few and small,
But all are cool and quiet-clean, uncluttered and at all times
      brightly lit. Perhaps it was the cardinal's guard that
      brought her here —

It grows like a weed in the courtyard, its hot-red
Bloom-spikes shooting up like rockets by the black screen doors.
Someone must have left those screen doors open and she flew in.
I found her perched on the fountain and because I did
Not know her right at first, had not yet come to understand
That freedom is unnatural, a curse, I misread her
Relief as desperation and I set her free.

           But how cruel it is to free a thing — to do so
Is to contradict the nature of that thing, to insure that thing's
      erasure. Our bonds define us, after all; they're what protect
      us from an earth cursed by hunger.
No wonder she flew from my shooing in frantic dashes and
      suicidal swoops! Those black doors standing open must
      have looked to her like her father's awful jaws pride
Wide by want. By the time I realized who it was,
It was too late. I'd chased her free and closed the doors behind
      her. Had I known, I might have let her stay. No —
I would have. I would have. Let her stay.

THE CONJUGAL BED

                                    The banyan trees
Are empty; great flocks of peach-faced lovebirds once

Roosted in them, allopreening and eating those berries
Swollen by the moist, August heat to an almost sexual

Bursting.

With nothing left to eat them, the berries fall and ripen
And split, spilling blood-colored pulp in thick, reeking

Streams that seep into the stump-holes where the palm
Trees used to be.

PART 3

MEDITATION ON BEETHOVEN: SYMPHONY 9

Another day of hair in my food.
Another day of being cheated, overlooked.

Another day of nausea.
I play Beethoven: Symphony 9.

The violin simmers for an instant,
And the cello simmers for an instant,
And the timpani,
The timpani comes crashing.

The sound says I am the hand of God.
The sound says I am the fist of God come crashing.

I recline,
No stranger to violence.

I survey my field of spiders,
My field of moths, my field of daffodils.
I spread my arms
As though over a great army.

Where is this God I've heard so much
About?

AND THE SUNFLOWER WEEPS FOR THE SUN, ITS FLOWER

1

There is a hole in the garden. It is empty. I envy it.

Emptiness: the only freedom there is
In a fallen world.

2

Father Sunflower, forgive me —. I have been so preoccupied with
    my backaches and my headaches,
With my sore back and my headaches and my beat-skipping heart,

I have ignored the subtle huzzah of the date palms and daisies, of
    the blue daze and the date palms —

3

                              Or don't forgive me, what do I care?
I am tired of asking for forgiveness; I am tired of being frightened
    all the time.
I want to run down the street with a vicious erection,
Impaling everything, screaming obscenities
And flapping my arms; *fuck the date palms,*
Fuck the daisies —

4

As a man, I am a disappointment, I know that.
Is it my fault I was born in shadow? Through the banyan trees,

An entourage of slovenly blondes
Comes naked and begging —

5

My days fly from me as though from a murderer.
Can you blame them?
Behind us, the house is empty and quiet as light.

What have I done, Mother,
That I should spend my life
Alone?

SELF-PORTRAIT WITH WHISKEY AND PISTOL

1

Of all the things this day turned out to be, a celebration of me
    was not one of them.

2

Maybe if I surrounded myself with prostitutes and strippers, my
    celibacy would feel less like a lack and more like an act
Of heroic self-denial.

3

My life and I live in the trees and share a tail.

4

Our stomach turns its peach pit to the moon!

5

Even if it's true, what they say, that love is never a waste of time
    no matter how impossible the object,

You wouldn't know it from living.
On this street.

6

How disappointing it all is!
The lemon trees, the banyan trees, the sky —
How disappointing it all is.

7

Look, the Great Poet of Solitude is pruning his roses!
(Even the way he does nothing is monstrous.)

8

O birds! O birds! Be not stingy with thy feathers white, I am
     washing my hands!

9

Cloudy or not, here I come —

MÉDITATION MALHEUREUSE

1

                The rain stops

Just long enough to make you think
Of the one day in your whole rotten
Childhood you were happy.

2

Then, it starts raining again.

BECAUSE THE PAST IS NEVER IN THE PAST AND BECAUSE IT IS MY BIRTHDAY

1

The road, how long and hard it looks this morning, like the time
    one spends in grammar school.

2

Like the gray and faded pages of a primer in which every lesson
Begins with "give" and ends with "up," these days at the wetter

End of November.

3

The wind blows and those crows, from the leafless trees
Of the park, take flight, their wings spreading like black

Cloth across the late-November sun, throwing the whole
World into coldness and shadow —

4

In The Schoolroom of Innumerable Sorrows,
My name floats in red ink on the blackboard.

On the black floor, in the moonlight, the outline of a body.

What is its name, that monster standing at the blackboard,
By the body, holding that red pen like it's a straight razor?

On the black floor, the moonlight is pooling.

THE WILDFLOWER FIELD

1

        Like fireworks, those wildflowers.
Fireflowers. Wildfires. The light

        Shining out like heat
From their yellow heads —, mind-

Blowing! Their petals, like sparks, falling,
Blowing through the field, setting

The grass on fire —

2

The starlit, wide southeastern sky
Seems paltry by comparison — as

If it were the afterthought, a field
Of second-rate fires burning cool

And passionless —

3

            So what if the moon's

Cold fusion throws a glowing on

The grass?
            Where's the crash —

That climax of diamonds, that wild, yellow
Crash of sparks

The wind will use to set this field
On fire?

OF PASSION AND SEDUCTIVE TREES

1

Jezebelian, all tongue,

I give you my only box of drop-dead plums;

a mason jar's glut

of those prissy figs you love; kiwis wrapped in burlap, tied with twine.

And quick narcotic clementines!

Clementines thick as rickshaws in Shanghai.

But those whiplash-magnificent trees,

those mango trees, those cherry trees, those trees unleashed with

tangerines:

I breathe, thistle of thistles,

in their immediate starlight.

2

In this immediate starlight,

I give you my only box of ox-eye mums;

a botanist's pot

of those drowsy buds you love; sweetpeas packed in sawdust crates,

roped fast.

And red electric fountain grass!

Such grass as shiftless rickshaws could not rut.

But these whiplashed, magnificent trees,

these orchid trees, these tulip trees, these trees unleashed with
    mescalbean:

I wished them in your eyes.

You weren't looking.

3

You are not looking —

so I give you my only box of hornet thrum;

an orchestra-let

of those katydids you love; termites locked in closets crammed
    with sticks.

And chic fantastic silverfish —

fish that skitter, rickshawed, over stone.

But for treed magnificence, whiplash,

for trumpet trees, for wahoo-trees, for trees unleashed with calabash:

for them, not you, am I

athletic, jezebelian, all tongue.

GREEN SQUALL

for Kimberly Johnson

Lightning —
Now there's a sexy machete: a pounce of sky electric —
    electricitied — inflamed.

             What's the sugar, Hurricane?

The rain tins its romantic in the water pots.

The waterspouts are full-on
Rashmahanic.

             What's the hurry, Sugarcane?

A pouncing sky enlightninged,
Edgy-sexed. . . .

This is the sugar.

This is the hurry.

JOY ON THE EDGE OF VERTIGO

1

Today I Will Risk What I Love

Mornings of maniacal elation; invincible strippers

And breadfruit; romantic ideas about women

It is wrong to kiss; mid-morning maniacal elation,

That fabulous, phosphorous, rapid fandango!;

Kiwis and kumquats and naked brunettes;

The romantic ideal so far as it concerns itself with sordid

Trampolines; this mid-morning's maniacal elation.

2

And How Will I Risk It?

I will speak at length with an idiot.

I will cadaver all my lovelies into grunts.

I will shimmy and breathe, O liquored anemones!

I will speak at length with an idiot.

I will prance in lavender, back-scratched.

I will harass anyone with owl, awl or ax.

I will speak at length with an idiot.

3

Today Will Risk What I Love

For so may I be Exquemellined, on the off-chance,

To thunder and violets, antiqued birdhouses,

Lascivious harpoonists, magpies.

For so may I be forever in maniacal elation!

This tease of rain and adventure, this swarm

Of impatient daisies, this beating heart,

For so may I be forever infested with angels.

FIRECRACKER CATALOGUE

Garden of Starlit Flowers

Flaming Chrysanthemum

Blue Umbrellas *(w/ report)*

All-Blooming Chandelier

Birds of Double Paradise

Happy Lightning Rocket

Innumerable Stars *(12 ct.)*

Bomb of Heaven Singing

Jumbo Christmas Missile

Jumping Monkey Candle

Pink Carnation Dynamite

Fountain of Silver Kisses

Emerald Parachutes *(7 ct.)*

Loudly Flowering Bower

Wall of Sunlit Butterflies

Repeating Beehives *(blue)*

Repeating Beehives *(gold)*

Bouquet of Wild Comets

Blessèd Festival Cannon

Blessèd Family Firebomb

AUBADE

1

Standing next to a large white pot
Filled to overflowing with orange

And yellow snapdragons, my old
Coonhound looks across the dew-

Strewn lawn at the magnolia tree.
Suddenly, from somewhere deep

Within the squall of all those big
And sloppy blossoms, a desolate

Call rings out.

2

         This morning, still
And warm, heavy with the smells

Of gardenia and Chinese wisteria,
The first few beams of spring sun-

Light filtering through the flower-
Crowded boughs of the magnolia,

I cannot conceive a more genuine,
More merciful, form of happiness

Than solitude.

3
In a single, black and ragged line,
The shadow of the magnolia tree

Draws nearer to the flower pots.
The coonhound lowers her snout

To its dark edge — . What was it
We heard call out so mournfully?

To what heartbreak would a call
Like that be heir? The air is still,

But differently.

THE WILDFLOWER FIELD

1

     Work-like,

They move their purple and white,
Red and yellow heads to the edge

Of the field and stand — leaf-deep —
In a seeping flood of fallen petals:

The wind is picking up.

2

When I say "work-like," I mean:
"Joylessly," "with a tremendous

Effort." How fitting this field is
In the state of Florida!

     Dark sky-
Lit fields full of aching flowers;

Fallen petals (the wind, picking
Up); has it always felt this way —

3

Like rain? Soon, the field will
Be rickety with drips. The red

Heads and the purple heads of
Those wildflowers, the yellow

Heads and the white heads of
Those wildflowers will droop

Into the mud and the flood of
Falling petals —

4

                  The dark skies
Getting darker, coming closer.

A BOOK OF COMMON DAYS

a supplemented cento

1

Not enough effort in the sky for morning.
The only relics left are those long,

Blunt fingers among the multitudinous buds.
How hard it is, we say —

The will to work is laid aside.

2

I have reached no conclusions, have erected no boundaries.
I have rested, drooling at the mouth-hole.

I have imagined bees coming and going.
I have said that the soul is not more than the body.

I've melted my silver for you.
I have strewn the leaf upon the sod.

I have just come down from my father.
I have suffered, in a dream, because of him.

3

Suddenly from all the green in the park,
A small white envelope appears.

As limpid, dense twilight comes,
The center of its patch of darkness, sparkling,

Rises like a moon made of black glass.
Beneath the clouds the low sky glows —

The garden that was never here,
Reveal it to me.

4

When the good and the violent are sleeping
When the city moon looks out on the streets

When the soul lies down in that grass
When spring comes back

When Judas writes the history of solitude
When I was young and miserable and pretty

When the green field comes off like a lid
When it prays —

5

I keep a blue bottle.
It convinces me I have seen my soul.

Where did they go, that couple I saw chasing a child
Around the side of the empty house across the street?

The sun is going down,
That fire that eats what it illuminates.

Dead leaves are falling in the dormant air.

6
The history of solitude is long.
It is like the history of twilight, the shadows

Of the birch trees lengthening,
The shadows of the gateposts

Lengthening, the Shadow of the Ploughman
Stretching out across the field —

7
What am I that my soul should hide from me?
From the evening fields, the black moon rose.

So fierce-some was that moon upon its rising,
It made the world on which it rose grow cold.

FEAST OF THE ASCENSION, 2004. PLANTING HIBISCUS

From being to being an idea, nothing comes through that intact.
Look at the garden: dew-swooned and with fat blooms swollen,
With shade leaf-laced beneath the lemon trees —

It is hard to believe beauty is the new ugliness.
But it must be, why else would so many of my contemporaries
    mock it so?

                    I guess it is true what they say —
That once a man falls he never again puts faith in the ground
On which he walks.

Putting faith in the ground —, is that what I am doing?
Is that what these blooms have been trying to tell me?
Is that what all their swooning
Has been about?

            The shade grows long. The shade grows long
Upon the lawns and the fat green leaves of these lemon trees
Are still in the early evening.

I could be buried here. That is,
I am — , I am buried.
Here.

NOTES

Out of These Wounds, the Moon Will Rise: "the single light shining at the center of all things" and "the dense[, eccentric] planets orbiting around it" come from Robert Bly's essay "Refusing to Be Theocritus" (*Neruda and Vallejo: Selected Poems* [Beacon, 1993]).

Of Hunger and Human Freedom: *cardinal's guard* (section 9) is a West Indian perennial.

The Conjugal Bed: *allopreening* is an ornithological term meaning *mutual preening*.

Green Squall: *rashmahanic* is West Indian Creole; it means *unruly* or *unruly behavior*.

Joy on the Edge of Vertigo: *Exquemellined* (section 3) refers to A. O. Exquemelin (1645–1707), a chronicler of buccaneers.